AF244641

Caught

and

Spanked

By

J. G. Knox

Love, Truth, & Life Publishing

215 Fuller Drive

Easley, SC 29640

United States

360-690-0842

This short story details a case of corporal punishment. Corporal punishment is a useful tool of correction. Nations teaching and using physical discipline have much lower rates of violent crime than nations that proscribe it. However, it cannot be used in anger or incorrectly with good results. It is a tool, not a philosophy. It is the purpose of this story is to illustrate the correct way to discipline. If you use spanking or paddling be sure you do it with love, the purpose of helping the recipient, not just punishing them, and never of hurting them.

ISBN   9781939159977

Caught

A deep voice on the phone, "Mrs. Johnson?"

I said, "Yes, do you know it is 11:30 at night?"

"Yes. This is Deputy O'Hollaran at the sheriff's office. Do you have a daughter, Carley Johnson?"

I sat down.

I said, "Yes."

"You need to come down and get her. We picked her up on Mill Pond Road."

Mill because there was a mill; pond because when the mill was running there was a pond; and road because there was a traveled road used by her father to check the water flow each shift for the four years. He was a lead man at the now closed mill. Now, Mill Pond Road is traveled only by lovers, and sheriff's deputies searching for young lovers doing things they should not be doing.

"Thank you, I'll be right there." I started to hang up. "Wait, where are you?"

I'd never been to the sheriff's office. This was the kind of thing Jim should be doing, but rarely does now. No work for him in our town after the mill shut down and a family to feed, he had to work. With two adults and six children, it took more than a job at Walmart. We needed money. Five years ago he got his commercial driver's license and has been driving long haul since then. Three weeks on the road then six days home, life is hard, harder than we wanted, but necessary if our children were to have a life.

Deputy O'Hollaran said, "Behind the court house, the corner of Washington and 2nd Street. Do you know where it is?"

"Yes, thank you."

30 minutes later, an embarrassed teenager in the passenger's seat, we headed home.

"Carley, what in the world were you doing on Mill Pond Road?"

A stupid question, I know, but one a Mother ask.

"We weren't doing anything, Momma. We were looking at the stars."

"That's what Deputy O'Hollaran said, lying on a blanket in the back of Bill's pickup looking at the stars. What was your dress doing tangled around your waist?"

Carley went silent.

"Well!" I said.

She was going to say something!

"Mom!---I, we weren't doing anything!"

"Kissing?"

"Yes. We were kissing."

"Your dress"?

"It sort of got tangled up. We were moving around."

"And where were his hands? Did his hands help it up?"

"Well---I didn't do anything, Momma."

"Have you"?

"No"!

"Would you have if Deputy O'Hollaran hadn't stopped you"?

"No"!

"Are you sure"?

"I'm a good girl, Momma," she whispered.

Could I hear her over the engine?

"I didn't hear you, Carley. Why are you whispering?"

"I'm a good girl, Momma," she whispered again.

"Are you a good girl because Deputy O'Hollaran stopped you"?

This time silence answered my question. I stopped, pulled off to the shoulder, and looked at her. Turning on the light inside the car, I wait for her to look at me.

She looked down. She looked out the window. She looked at her feet---everywhere except to her left hand side---and me.

"Well"?

"I'm sorry, Momma. I really am. We didn't do anything!"

"Have you done anything"?

"No, Mom, I'm a virgin. OK!"

She was talking, defending herself. She was a good girl. I knew she was a good girl, or hoped I knew she was a good girl. In our church virginity is expected, valued, and encouraged. She knew our values: what her father and I expected of her.

I put the car in drive and looked back; nothing coming, I pulled out.

"We need to talk more when we get home," I said.

A short drive, our town is small, big enough for one high school, two grammar schools, two supermarkets, a once prosperous downtown replaced by a Walmart, three blocks from our house, and a lover's lane, Mill Pond Road.

I pushed the button on the garage door opener. We were home.

"Everybody's asleep, Carley. Let's go in the study."

"Momma, we didn't do anything"!

She followed me, more emotional this time. She knew what a talk in the study meant. Jim's study, he used it for writing. A history major, his hobby was writing historical fiction. In his absence, I used it for my sewing room. For the children it was a quiet room, unless a child was ordered to the study. A command to go to the study was for something serious, something they did not want to discuss, something wrong. Then the privacy was not for quiet, but crying. Under Jim's desk hung the paddle.

Never leaving the study, the paddle was a gift from Jim's Sunday school teacher. He designed it from a thick, soft piece of leather. A flexible impact, it never bruised and imparted more heat over a larger area than a wooden paddle. Steam vents through several rows of neatly trimmed holes concentrating heat, leaving small, round, rapidly disappearing blisters, a reminder to young buttock owners of their misdeeds. A handle triple folded and stitched for control, the paddle was a craftsman's tool for giving pain and avoiding injury.

It came out for Carley's benefit on its first outing, four years and seven months ago. Almost a teenager, she needed a more intense paddling than the hand swats required by her younger siblings. Wiping dust from it before paddling her, years of accumulation came off on the moist cloth. Was I being a good mother, not wanting to use a dirty paddle on my girl, or trying to put off the inevitable? I knew she needed the paddle to change her behavior. I didn't want to use it.

As I rubbed off the last of the dust, she said, "Momma, you don't have to paddle me. Why don't you ground me or something?"

"What you did was yell at me in the kitchen for the forth time today. If I ground you, you will be yelling at me until your grounding is over. Besides, it's clean now."

"Momma," she said looking at the paddle.

"I know you're a good girl, Carley. I know you are upset because your father is not here, and doing things you wouldn't do, if he were."

I put my hand on her shoulder and said, "It has to stop, Honey."

Her hands shaking, she bent over Jim's desk. As disrespectful as she was in the kitchen, she needed a good cry. She needed the paddle to give her a good cry.

My first time using a paddle, I was as nervous as my daughter. Did she need two pops or ten? I didn't want to hurt her, had to give her enough pain to cry and change her behavior. Two solid pops and tears dripped on Jim's table. With the third and forth, she let loose, sobbed. I stopped. She kept crying.

"Carley, are you going to stop yelling at me"?

"Yes, Momma"

"I know you'll do better, be the girl your Daddy and I raised you to be. I love you, Carley."

"I'm sorry, Momma."

"Carley, why don't you stay in here till you get your crying out, and while you're here, the paddle is too dried out. The leather is cracking. Put a coat of linseed oil on it before putting it away, OK?"

"Yes, Momma"

"Carley, you will do better, or you'll have another paddling. It's up to you." I kissed her forehead, she hugged me. I went back to the kitchen.

Four of them old enough for its use now, and my role strained by Jim's absence, dusting was over. I stop having the children oil it two months ago after her brother, Bob, needed a paddling. It put an oil stain on the back of his blue jeans. Blisters, a three-day reminder of his sin, useful; oil stains with blister holes on his jeans, the imprint of the paddle, not a good thing, I poured half my remaining stain remover on those jeans before washing them.

This time in the study, I sat on Jim's desk facing my daughter. She stood on the carpet trembling. I shook with anger. The paddle hung on its nail. Being under the desk, waiting to come out, the paddle added tension to our conversation, added an octave to Carley's pleas.

"Mom, we didn't do anything"!

"Carley, you were in the back of a pickup, laying down, your dress up with a young man."

She glanced up at me then looked down at her feet.

"Carley, let's say a prayer before we say anything else, OK? Do you want to start?" I held her hands.

"I'm sorry, God---Is there anything else you want me to say, Momma?"

To Carley, I said, "No, it's OK, Carley." To God, I say, "Thank you, God. Carley is all right." I squeezed her hands. "God, I know she is a good girl who made a mistake, and I know you will help her do better. God, I ask you to help us. I'm her mother and I need your help to help her. Please guide me, us, tonight."

I let her hands go.

I said, "Carley, do I understand how you feel?"

She glanced up at me. I was an old woman, almost 36. How could I understand how she feels?

I said, "I understand, Carley. I'm a woman."

She looked up at me holding my gaze for a minute before looking back down. Did she believe I knew how she felt?

"Carley, did it feel good to be kissing him, to have him running his hand up your dress, to be lying close to him feeling him breathe"?

"Momma"!

"It did, didn't it"?

"Momma"!

Were these things to be talked about with a mother?

"I know how you feel, Carley. Last month, when your brothers, sister, and you went to youth conference staying over at a motel with the group from church, your Dad and I stayed home. I know how you feel."

"Momma"!

She looks me straight in the eyes.

Her eyes say without words, *You're wrong to be talking to me about this sort of thing. You're too old to feel the things I'm feeling, to know the wants I want.*

"Carley, your Dad and I were in each other's arms on the Hammock in the back yard watching the stars. He touched me, he held me like Bill was holding you. It felt so good. My dress rode up. We came back inside. We did everything you were feeling like doing. He made love to me. It felt wonderful, Carley. It is the most wonderful feeling a woman can have, except---"

She looked at me with a stern look again. She thought, *Except what?*

I answered, "Carley, except when I held you in my arms the first time at the hospital, your Daddy beaming a smile at me. Then he took you and the doctors finished working with me. He brought you back and put you in my arms. You nursed me. I went to sleep holding you. That's the except, Carley. When I had you, when I had your brothers and sisters, being a mother is the most wonderful feeling a woman can have."

She kept looking at me. I knew how she felt. She knew I knew how she felt.

I looked deep in her eyes. She was yet to know the joy of sexual fulfillment. It showed in her eyes. I breathed a sigh of relief.

"Mom, I want to have children," she said.

"Now"?

"No, not now. When I'm married, like you and Dad."

"That's what I want, Carley. I want to be a grandmother, but I don't want my grandchildren with you to be named Johnson (our surname). Do you understand?"

"We didn't do anything, Momma"!

"Carley, that night, when you were at the youth conference, your Dad and I were home alone with your younger two sisters, Amy and Linda. They were asleep. Do you think I could have gotten off our hammock and gone to bed without making love to your father?"

She looked at me. Why was I asking her?

"Carley, making love is the most wonderful feeling, but it's one with peaks of intensity for a woman. Two weeks after your period, intensity and desire are so strong even good girls can't resist. That weekend with your father was very special. It was two weeks after my period. I couldn't have stopped if I wanted to stop."

I wanted to share.

"Carley, I missed my last period. I won't know for another month, but I think I'm pregnant. I feel like I am."

Tension broke.

Carley smiled, gave me a hug. "Wonderful, Momma."

I held her asking, "Carley, when was your period." I know. I bought her sanitary pads. "Two weeks ago wasn't it, Carley?"

She looked down.

"Carley, you're in midcycle. Do you know how hard it is for a girl to stop when she's in midcycle?"

I looked at her. She looked down. She knew.

"Carley, if Deputy O'Hollaran hadn't stopped you, what would have happened?"

"Momma---" she never finished.

"I know, Honey. I understand. I'm a woman too. Your Dad and I don't believe in birth control. The church teaches against it, and even if they didn't, we don't believe in it. We've never used it. I've never taken a birth control pill. The most wonderful thing in our lives are you and your brothers and sisters. We want children. If I'm pregnant, it is a blessing from God---I want to be in the hospital in eight months having another baby. I want you to be with me this time, to stay with me through the whole process."

She smiled, wanted to be with me, was excited to be a big sister again.

"Really, Momma, you'll let me be with you?"

"Of course, and I want to be with you when you have your babies, only not now, Carley."

We hugged.

"Carley, I know how you feel. I know how good it feels to pet, to make love, to be a woman. You know part of it. The rest you have to save for marriage. Marriage makes what I and your father did, and do, absolutely right. I want you to make love, to have the feelings I have."

"Yes, Momma."

"Are you sorry for what you and Bill did tonight?"

She looked at me.

I had seen worry. I had seen fear that she was in trouble. Had I seen one inkling of sorry in her tonight?

"You're not sorry, Carley. You're a young woman feeling passion. I understand."

"Momma, I know we went too far. I'm sorry," she said looking up at me, then looking down.

"You're not, Carley. You need to be. It is important if you're going to stay pure."

"I'm sorry, Momma. I just have trouble showing it sometimes."

"I understand, Carley."

I broke our hug getting to my feet and hugging her again. Reaching under the desk, she knew what I was doing.

"Momma"!

I lifted the leather loop on the end of the paddle and brought it out.

"You don't have to paddle me, Momma. I'm sorry."

"You're not sorry, Honey. You need to be, but you're not."

"Momma"!

She knew I was right. In her eyes, I saw no tears, not one, nor should there have been. She was a normal high school girl, doing what normal high school girls do and will be a normal, pregnant high school girl, unless she puts the brakes on her feelings with feeling. The paddle would help her feel the regret she needs to feel.

"Honey, I'm not mad at you. I don't want to do this, but you have to feel sorrow to make the changes you need to make."

She looked at the paddle, looked at the desk.

"Momma, I need to go to the bathroom. Can I go to the bathroom first?"

"Sure, Honey. Don't take long. We need to get to bed."

I understood how she felt. I understood passion. I understood love. I understood she must feel regret, or she would fulfill her passion, ruin her life. I looked at the paddle, rubbed it with my hand. A few minutes ago, I ached to bring it out and use it. Breathing in, a different feeling filled me. She needed paddling. I loved her. I hated to see her cry and knew she must. It was either paddle her or get her birth control. Against our beliefs, she had to learn restraint. I patted the paddle wanting to put it under the desk again.

She came back closing the door.

NOT FOR GETTING CAUGHT

"Are you ready?" I said..

"Momma, you don't have to paddle me. I'm sorry. I know I was wrong. I won't do it again."

"Do what again?"

"Get caught with Bill making out on Mill Pond Road."

"I'm glad you got caught, Honey. Getting caught isn't the reason I'm paddling you."

"What"?

"You need paddling for petting, making out in a private place where you have no control of yourself or what happens. Getting caught isn't the reason. What you did is the reason. Getting caught only brought your actions to my attention. Now, why do you need a paddling?"

She said, "For petting, making out in a private place---what else?"

"Lets keep it short, petting, doing it in a place and time you shouldn't have. Clear enough?"

"Petting, doing it in a place and time I shouldn't have. Is that it Momma?"

We had a ritual: one to make sure the child focused on their error. What she had in her mind during the paddling and as pain opened her heart to correct the wrong, must be her mistake. Her crime in her mind as the pain started set the cause of her pain, not me giving it, not Deputy O'Hollaran for catching her, but her own correctable actions.

"I don't know, Carley. Do you? That's the gist of it, but I want you to tell me why petting is wrong, and why the time and place was wrong."

I put the paddle down and waited for her answer. I wanted her to repeat back to me what she did wrong with clarity before we started.

"What do you want me to say, Momma?"

I picked up the paddle.

"Lean over the desk, Carley. Keep your hands on the desk until I tell you we are done. If you need more paddling, if you think I should start the paddling over from the beginning, take your hands off the desk, then we will start again. Go over the reasons for your paddling before we do it, and tell me during your paddling what you did wrong when I ask. When it's over, you owe me, and yourself, an apology for what you did. Understood?"

"I'm sorry, Momma," She said leaning over the desk.

"Break it in parts. What is wrong with petting?"

"It gets me excited, makes me want to have sex?"

"Pretty close. Is it wrong to be excited and wanting to have sex?"

"Yes."

"Is it wrong for your father and I to get excited with each other and want to have sex"?

She says, "It's right for you and Daddy."

I say, "Is it wrong for you?"

She says, "It's wrong for me."

I say, "Why?"

She says, "Because you're married. You're supposed to have sex with each other. If you didn't, I wouldn't be here."

"What about you? Is it wrong for you to want sex?"

"Yes."

"Is it? You're a normal girl. Girls want sex. Normal enough, but---You tell me; what is wrong with you wanting sex?"

She says, "I'm not married?"

I say, "Yes. It's normal for you to want it, but you need to keep that want inside you for a few more years until you get married, and then turn it loose. Then it'll be wrong for you not to be getting excited and having sex. If you come home and are having trouble with your husband and not having sex with him, we'll come back in here and I'll give you a paddling for not petting, not getting excited, and not having sex. It's your timing that's wrong, not the desire. Do you understand?"

"Yes, Momma, it's my timing. Is bad timing enough reason to paddle me?"

I said, "Yes, your timing can get you pregnant, give you a baby without a father---make you an unwed mother. A tragedy for the baby and you. You were doing what God made you to do: doing it at the wrong time and place, something a paddling will help you avoid in the future."

I move behind her. I square my stance with her bottom. I put the paddle on her cheeks.

"I'm sorry, Momma. Please!"

She looked back at me pleading, hoping.

I said, "Tell me why you're being paddled?"

"For petting before I'm married," she said looking at her hands, not looking back.

I pivoted, bringing the paddle off her bottom, up.

Crack, the paddle bounced off her bottom, sounded like a shot. I caught it, brought it up, brought it down. Crack, an echo off the wall, crack, crack, crack---five hard swats, I paused. Her whimpers muffled by the cracks and echoes of cracks replaced silence with pain. She was crying.

Moving to her other side, not wanting all the blisters and heat on her left buttock, the paddle hit hardest on the side opposite it's handle, I asked, "Carley, what did you do wrong?"

"Pppetting and not being married"!

Resilience in her voice, she handled the pain, wasn't finished, needed more intensity.

Squaring my stance again, I gave her five more swats.

"Carley, what did you do wrong?"

"Pppppetting an---"

She broke down in tears sobbing unable to finish, unable to control the pain. The pain controlled her. The message, the thoughts in her mind at this moment filled her, penetrated deep into her long term memory, created an association with pain and petting in the wrong place and time, something permanent, life changing: something that would never have happened without the paddle.

I finished for her, "and not being married, Carley?"

She nodded her head, tears streaming down her face.

I put the paddle down, turned her to me, and wrapped my arms around her.

"That's right, Carley, petting, doing it at the wrong time and place---and not being married."

She dropped her head on my shoulder sobbing, "I'm sorry, Momma!"

She understood what she did wrong, and regretted it.

Now for correction.

"I know, Honey. You won't do it again will you?"

"No, Momma!"

She shook crying with a steady whine. The pain in her bottom burned and would burn like it was on fire for another twenty minutes.

I sat her down to talk, not that she felt like sitting, but it kept her bottom warm, kept her focus on her paddling, correction, and change.

"Carley, you were paddled to help you change your thinking and behavior. What can you do to make sure it doesn't happen again?

She was trembling. "I don't know, Momma."

It was difficult for her to think when her oral temperature was 98.7 degrees and the thin, very pain sensitive, layer of skin over her buttocks was over 110 degrees, but it was the time she must think about it.

"Carley, you're human; you need a life. What can you live with? What kind of rules do we need so you can have a normal life and avoid situations like tonight? You can't kiss in the back of a pickup truck on Mill Pond Road. Where do you think it is safe for you to be able to have a kiss and not risk going too far?"

"I don't know, Momma," she said.

109 degrees, a few degrees cooler and her thinking would move back between her ears.

"Tell me, Carley, where do you think is safe?"

"At a church party?"

"I guess. It depends on the party, but yes, good. Where else?"

"At home, in the house."

"Good idea, Carley. With me and your brothers and sisters around is perfect. Any place else?"

"Is the movies OK, Momma?"

"Not the drive-in."

"Why else would kids go to the drive-in, Momma"?

"Yes, I remember. If you go to the drive-in, go to watch the movie!"

"Momma"!

Her buttocks and her thinking were approaching normal teenage temperature.

"It's up to you. If I get a call reporting you petting in the drive-in, saying you're in the back seat of a car watching the movie, or your head is below the dash, you know what can happen.

"I understand exactly what you did, and why you did it. I was your age once. I understand the feelings you have, and respect them. I respect you. I know you're a good girl and will be a good girl all your life. I love you and am proud to be your mother."

"I knew you were going to paddle me the minute I saw Deputy O'Hollaran's flashlight shining in my eyes, Momma."

Carley settled in my arms, hugged me again, said, "Momma, I have to go to sleep. It's late."

"Good night. I'm glad you're my daughter."

"Good night, Momma."

I listened to her close her door. She was not crying.

I should dropped right off to sleep; I couldn't.

I thought of Jim. He was probably driving. It's easier at night he told me, less traffic. I wished he were home, and he would be---if it weren't for me.

When we met, I was in my first semester, my freshman year at state, a wild-eyed high school girl on her first trip away from home without my parents. They dropped me off at my dorm. Momma cried on her way back to their car. Excited, feeling her apron stings fall away, I was ready to be on my on. I didn't cry until two day later when the missing of her started. Watching them leave standing on the lawn waving goodbye, I saw a boy come out of the other dorm. He saw me, waved at me, not seeing my parents car fading around the science building, he thought I was waving at him. I kept waving at him, put my hand to my lips, not knowing him. What was I doing? I rushed back in the dorm.

I saw him again that night at the cafeteria. I smiled at him. He smiled a wonderful smile at me, toothy, with deep sincere eyes hidden behind murky lenses. He approached my table.

He said, "Can I sit here?"

There were only three hundred other empty seats, we were at the college the day before classes started, almost an empty campus. He took me on a walkabout around the campus. The lady from admissions had already taken me and my parents on a complete tour twice, once when I applied and again after I was accepted. A three hour drive from the only bed I had slept in since I was five years old, I wanted a closer look at the place I was going to be sleeping for four years. I asked questions as if I had never been in the men's dorm---even if it was only the lobby.

Sitting looking out the glass front on the couch by me, he pointed out the administration building.

He said, "I work here Tuesday and Thursday afternoon at the dean of student's office. I remembered. He was there on my second visit, but herded along with a group of four other high school seniors and our parents, he was part of the furniture. Now I was interested, not in the building, or the dean's office---him.

He looked like a movie star, James Dean, he was like James Dean, a lot of the same facial features, eyes, nose, nice hair, a wonderful smile, thin, short, a pretty body, and thick glasses. I stopped him between buildings, took his glasses away.

I said, "Did anyone ever tell you, you look like James Dean without your glasses?"

He said, "I look like him with them on too. If he had been wearing his glasses when he was driving up the coast, he wouldn't be dead."

Blind as a bat without his glasses, good enough vision to drive a truck with them on, he could never have been a pilot, and never considered any job that required that kind of vision. In his junior year, in one year and nine months and he would be a history teacher. I wasn't sure what I was going to be, maybe a home economics teacher. Studying, freshman English, history, and physical education would start Wednesday. No classes, no other students around, we had Tuesday.

After the administration building, science building, humanities building, and foot ball field, he showed me Adam's hill, a small rise above the campus on undeveloped land. We watched the sun settling passed the administration building dome. He kissed me. I kissed him. It was the best campus tour I ever had. The next day we toured the town, had sodas at the malt shop.

He said, "Friday night?"

I said, "Unhuh."

Our first official date was on a Friday night then he took me out every Friday night for a month, and he met me in the cafeteria for lunch most days.

Like most working-class students, he was broke, working his way through school with a part time job on campus at the college and another one nights off campus pumping gas at the Esso station half a mile from his dorm. He had no car. We had no privacy, stealing kisses on Adam's hill within sight of the whole college one of the deans pointed us out, mentioned us in freshman orientation the next day. I blushed. We tried kissing on the back row of the theater in town, that didn't work. An older couple huffed, got up, and moved forward. On the nature walk at the bottom of the hill below the humanities building, Carl, his roommate, caught us, said, "Hi, Jim," just as he was pulling me tight to him for a deeper kiss. Pay back, Jim borrowed Carl's vintage station wagon to take me to the drive in two weeks before Thanksgiving break. We started kissing as soon as we were parked on the back row and Jim put the speaker in the window. After the show we didn't watch, we drove toward college. The sky was crystal clear; a million stars twinkled at us. I wanted to stop and look at them---

He said, "You didn't tell me you were a virgin. I wouldn't have---"

"I'm sorry," I said. "I want you to be happy with me."

"What is wrong with being a virgin? Guys marry virgins."

"You want to marry a virgin?"

"Well, yeah, don't most guys want to marry a virgin?"

I began to cry.

"I don't want any other guy, ever. I want you! You're the only guy I have made love too, or ever want to make love to me. I didn't know you wanted to marry a virgin!"

"I'm sorry," he said and kissed me.

I kept crying.

All the girls were talking about having sex with their boy friends. I adored him. I was afraid if I didn't; I would lose him.

"I want you, only you," I kissed him again.

He said, "I want you too."

We made love three more times and drove back to school.

The next day we met. He smiled. He kept dating me. He felt the same way about me; I felt about him. He wanted only me.

I thought, *I'd better get some pills.*

The doctor at the campus clinic gave me a prescription. I was starting them after my next period and to stay on them. The Doctor was unconcerned. With birth control, it didn't matter if I was active or not, sex would be safe; as long as, I was regular about taking my pills.

Putting the pills in my drawer, I waited. I didn't have my next period or the next. I went back to the doctor---pregnant. The doctor didn't ask, he set me up for an abortion the next week.

"I'm pregnant, Jim," I said.

"Weren't you on the pill?"

"I got some. I got them after we made love. I was supposed to start them after my next period. I'm sorry."

Tears raced down my cheeks.

"The doctor set me up for an abortion next week."

Jim glared at me.

"An abortion! You're going to abort our baby!"

Did I know him? In the middle of the sexual revolution, Jim was willing, but was it what he wanted? With me, he assumed I knew what I was doing; sex was what I wanted. He was trying to please me; as much as, I was trying to please him. He went to church Sundays, wanted to marry a virgin, and believed in our baby's right to life.

I said, "I don't want an abortion. I want our baby!"

I cried.

We married at a justice of the peace's office the day I was supposed to abort Carley.

His roommate loaned Jim enough money for a week's rent on a small room off campus. Keeping eating in the cafeteria, we had semester meal tickets, tried to survive. His father helped us with rent the rest of the term. My parents paid for our room the next term. Keeping up our health insurance, my Mom and Dad were disappointed in me, but helped us. Carley was born two days after finals.

Was there money for him to finish his last year? With a new baby was there any way I could continue school or work? Getting Jim a job at the mill, his dad helped. His father was on the production line in the mill for forty years before retiring. The plant manager assumed Jim would likely be working on the same production line till he retired or got promoted. Everything went well for eleven years. Jim moved up, was a lead man for four years and had been a foreman for two weeks when the mill closed. Without qualifications, Jim couldn't get another job. Using what savings we had, he trained to drive a truck and has been driving ever since.

Driving by the school two years after we married, pregnant with Joey, I recognized the old station wagon. His room mate got a job teaching history at Jim's high school. He is with the school system today and likely never will have another employer. Schools rarely close their doors and sell their desks, blackboards, and chalk to big international schools in China. Jim and he remain friends. Taking Carl out riding last summer, Jim told me Carl thought being on a big rig is an adventure.

Carley didn't know anything about this. We told her, we fell in love and got married. We never told her why her father didn't finish college or any of the rest. We'd tell her after she married.

My mother wasn't there to stop me, but I remember. I was a senior in high school, out petting, and came home at 1:00 AM. Did she ever give me a lecture! I avoided staying out late after that. She told me no petting. I promised her I wouldn't, went to bed with dry eyes, and slipped into bed without a tear. I kept my word until college---and Jim. Would I have been petting with Jim and slipped my panties off as I did, had I had an emotional, heart felt, crying episode with my mother over petting?

I drifted off to sleep, knowing Carley did not know my history, know how I wish I had been paddled. If I had lived as Jim really wanted and married as a virgin, her father would be principal of the high school, not Carl. She went to sleep missing her father and crying because of the paddle. I went to sleep crying and missing him because of the lack of it.

She slept in. I, the mother of five other kids, was up bleary eyed fixing breakfast. She got up for lunch; hugged me.

"Momma, I'm sorry. I was wrong. I needed paddling."

I smiled.

"Momma, you were right last night. If Deputy O'Hallaran hadn't come when he did---Bill would have made love to me. Momma, you corrected my feelings, thank you, but Deputy O'Holleran---he saved me. If he had not come up the road when he did I wouldn't be a virgin. I could be pregnant!"

"I'm sorry, Momma. Thank you."

"How do you feel about Deputy O'Hollaran this morning?"

"How can I ever thank him, Momma?"

"Carley, being a police officer is a thankless job. Most people yell at them, are mad at them for correcting them, and never say anything nice to them. I have an idea. We've the fixings for a pecan pie. Do you want to fix him one and take it down to the sheriff's office tonight when he comes on shift?"

She smiled.

That evening our station wagon made another trip to the sheriff's office. Saturday night, the busiest night of the week, he looked at us. The light went out of his eyes.

Did he think, *They are going to complain*?

"Deputy O'Hollaran, Carley fixed this pie for you," I said as she came in, after getting it out of the car.

She said, "I shouldn't have been on Mill Pond Road, Deputy O'Hollaran, I was wrong. You saved me from ruining my life. Thank you!"

Carley put the pie on his desk and hugged him.

The big man, shocked, almost fell backwards out of his chair then patted her on the back.

"Do you know how long it has been since anyone said thank you to me for doing my job?"

"No, but Carley and I are grateful. Thank you," I said.

"Thank you," he said.

He and the other deputy on shift took a slice each before taking it to the refrigerator.

"I'm going to keep this for the day shift and let them have some. Thank you again for coming back to tell me."

I said, "Deputy O'Hollaran, you asked last night if I have a daughter, Carley Johnson. Yes, I have a daughter, Carley Johnson. She's a good girl." I thought, *Thank you,* and put my arm around her shoulder as we walk out of the sheriff's office.

The End?

Not likely, pen on paper then printing press on paper, that is permanent, the end, or at least the end until the next edition. On-off bits of information stored in computers are changeable, meant to be changed. Send a hard copy of your changes or suggestions, and we will look at them, make needed changes. In the mean time we have published a number of stories and books on line and in paper. If you have thoughts to improve the work, write or call us, 360-690-0842.

Other Books, Short Stories, and Novellas by J G Knox

Love Thine Enemas and Heal Thyself
8th Edition
When the Jonquils Bloom Again
6th Edition
The Good Enema
3rd Edition
Marisa
3rd Edition
all available in kindle and in print
at
Amazon.com

To be placed on the mailing list for new publications, or to share observations about this book, or other books or papers we have written, please write:

Love Truth and Life Publishing
215 Fuller Drive
Easley, SC 29640

Or
Call
360-690-0842

We reprint books with corrections periodically and appreciate anything that will make future editions better. Those submitting corrections we use will be sent a new copy of the next edition.